Listening to Music

Elements Age 7+

Compiled and written by Helen MacGregor
Recording produced by Stephen Chadwick
Illustrations by Alison Dexter

A & C Black · London

Contents

DURATION

What you need to know about duration
  page 4
Listening links with the other recordings 4

Unsquare dance

What you need to know about the music 6
Activity 1: Sevens 6
Activity 2: Unsquare ostinatos 7
Activity 3: Sevens improvisation 8

Inspector Morse

What you need to know about the music 10
Activity 1: Di daa di daa 10
Activity 2: Secret agents 11

First published 1996 by A & C Black Publishers Ltd
37 Soho Square, London W1D 3QZ
www.acblack.com
Reprinted 2000, 2002

Text ©Helen MacGregor
Sound recording © A & C Black
Illustrations © Alison Dexter
Cover illustration © Jane Tattersfield
Edited by Sheena Roberts
Sound engineering by Stephen Chadwick
Post-production by Simon Kahn
Printed in Great Britain by Lavenham Press Ltd, Suffolk

A & C Black uses paper produced with elemental
chlorine-free pulp, harvested from managed sustainable forests.

DYNAMICS

What you need to know about dynamics 13
Listening links with the other recordings 13

Baris gede 'bandrangan'

What you need to know about the music 14
Activity 1: Listening box 14
Activity 2: Stand up sit down 15
Activity 3: Dynamic drum 16

TEMPO

What you need to know about tempo 18
Listening links with the other recordings 18

Winds on the mountain

What you need to know about the music 19
Activity 1: Traffic lights 20
Activity 2: Wind dance 22

Baris gede 'bandrangan'

What you need to know about the music 24
Activity 1: Listening box 24
Activity 2: Gamelan 24

TIMBRE

What you need to know about timbre 26
Listening links with the other recordings 26

La Volta

What you need to know about the music 28
Activity 1: Performing La Volta 29

Tomorrow the fox

What you need to know about the music 32
Activity 1: Match up voices 33
Activity 2: Match up memory 34
Activity 3: Singing Tomorrow the fox 35
Activity 4: Scrap band sort out 36
Activity 5: Tomorrow the fox finale 37
Activity 6: Something old something new 37

TEXTURE

What you need to know about texture 38
Listening links with the other recordings 38

Five pieces for orchestra, no 1

What you need to know about the music 40
Activity 1: Listening box 40
Activity 2: Night music 44

Dis long time, gal

What you need to know about the music 43
Activity 1: Steel pans 44
Activity 2: One two many 44
Activity 3: Texture twist 46
Activity 4: One two many with instruments 46
Activity 5: A new twist 46

Track list

PITCH

What you need to know about pitch 48
Listening links with the other recordings 48

Didlan

What you need to know about the music 49
Activity 1: Pitch in 49
Activity 2: Singing snakes and ladders 50

Stamping tubes

What you need to know about the music 52
Activity 1: Tapping tubes 52
Activity 2: Pitch walls 54

STRUCTURE

What you need to know about structure 56
Listening links with the other recordings 56

Rondeau

What you need to know about the music 58
Activity 1: Rondeau dance 58

Kartal

What you need to know about the music 60
Activity 1: Rhythm rondo 60
Activity 2: Concentration rondo 61
Activity 3: Animal elements rondo 62

Listening music

track
5   Unsquare dance   *page 7, 8, 39, 56*
11   Inspector Morse   *10, 11, 57*
16   Baris gede 'bandrangan'   *14, 24, 57*
18   Winds on the mountain   *13, 22, 48, 56*
20   La Volta   *29, 48, 56*
21   La Volta   *5, 29, 48, 56*
30   Tomorrow the fox   *4, 37, 38, 56*
31   Five pieces for orchestra, no 1   *13, 27*
35   Dis long time, gal   *18, 45, 56*
37   Didlan   *4, 27, 38, 49*
38   Stamping tubes   *55*
39   Rondeau   *18, 58*
42   Kartal   *5, 26, 61*

Children's reference

track
12   Morse code letters   *10*
13   Crack the code   *10*
14   Communication copy song   *11*
15   Communication backing track *11*
19   Gamelan   *24*
23   Match up memory card 1   *34*
24   Match up memory card 2   *34*
25   Match up memory card 3   *34*
26   Match up memory card 4   *34*
27   Tomorrow the fox copy song and
     backing track   *35*
28   Scrap band sort out backing track   *36*
29   Paper, plastic, wood, metal   *36*
32   Steel pans   *44*
36   Winds on the mountain pitch
     shape   *48*

Teacher's reference

track
1   Syncopation   *4*
2   Clapping syncopation   *5*
3   Fives and sevens   *6*
4   Counting in sevens with Unsquare
     dance   *7*
6   Bass ostinato   *7*
7   Syncopated clapping ostinato   *8*
8   Combined ostinatos   *8*
9   Bass ostinato on tuned instruments   *8*
10   Sevens improvisation   *9*
15   Communication song with
     morse code   *11*
17   Dynamic drum   *16*
22   Performing the music of La Volta   *29*
28   Scrap band sort out   *36*
33   Peel head john crow   *44*
34   One two many   *45*
40   Rondeau dance steps   *59*
41   Rhythm rondo   *60*
43   Concentration rondo   *61*

DURATION

What you need to know about duration

Music is made up of sounds and silences of different lengths. Groupings of sounds and silences make rhythms. Pulse, beat and metre are used to regulate time in music. All are aspects of duration.

Pulse, beat and metre

Music often has a regular beat – like the steady tap of walking feet. When the beat is not audible, it can be perceived as a silent pulse, like a silently swinging pendulum behind the music.

The beat of music can be organised into metre, a regular grouping of beats with the emphasis on beat 1, eg.

2 metre:	**1**	2	**1**	2	**1**	2	**1**	2	
3 metre:	**1**	2	3	**1**	2	3	**1**	2	3
5 metre:	**1**	2	3	4	5	**1**	2	3	4	5

Some beats within the metre may be regularly accented, so that they are felt more strongly than others, eg.

4 metre:	**1**	2	**3**	4	**1**	2	**3**	4
6 metre:	**1**	2	3	**4**	5	6	**1**	2	3	**4**	5	6

Syncopation

When a beat, which is usually weak, is instead accented, the effect is called syncopation:

Regular				Syncopated			
1	2	**3**	4	1	**2**	3	**4**

Reference track 1 gives you two examples of syncopation: a syncopated backing, and a syncopated melody.

Ostinato

A pattern of sounds which is repeated throughout a piece of music is called an ostinato, which literally means obstinate. In both pieces of music in this section, ostinato is used extensively.

In **Unsquare dance**, the children will be finding out how the composer has used syncopation within a metre of seven beats to make an exciting piece of music, which they can perform.

In **Inspector Morse**, they will be investigating rhythm in closer detail by making up their own patterns of long sounds, short sounds and silences.

Listening links with the other recordings

Explore this link with the children before or after the section on *Unsquare dance*.

> **Listen to track 30 Tomorrow the fox and track 37 Didlan**
>
> *Exploring metre*
> Ask the children to tap fingers on palms to mark the pulse. Can they discover how the pulse is grouped in each of these pieces? (*Tomorrow the fox* is grouped in twos and *Didlan* in threes.) Can the children suggest some different ways to move which will clearly identify the metre, eg.
>
>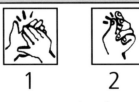
>
> | 1 | 2 |
> |---|---|
> | To - morrow the fox will | |
>
> | 1 | 2 | 3 |
> |---|---|---|
> | Dee | dee | dee diddle |

Explore these links before or after either section.

Listen to track 21 La Volta

Exploring ostinato
This version of *La Volta* starts with a pattern of three different low notes repeated again and again on the harpsichord with the left hand. This ostinato continues throughout while the recorder and right hand harpsichord part interweave the melody.

Before you listen to the piece, choose one child to play the ostinato on a tuned instrument.

Pulse	1	2	3	1	2	3	
		D	G		D	G	*repeat about eight times*
	G			G			

Questions you might ask
What did you notice about the pattern (Shelley) played? (It was only three notes played again and again. It didn't change. It was an ostinato.)

Now listen to *La Volta.*

What did you notice about La Volta? (The same pattern was played all through. It was the ostinato (Shelley) played.)

Listen to track 42 Kartal

Exploring syncopation
This piece is made up of syncopated rhythm patterns within a regular, four-beat metre. The first pattern is repeated many times during the piece, interspersed by other patterns.

As they listen to track 42, ask the children to count quietly in fours to establish the regular pulse. They can tap fingers on palms, making beat 1 stronger than 2, 3 and 4. (You can hear the pulse at the beginning of reference **track 2**.) Listen carefully – the pulse speeds up very slightly during the piece!

Questions you might ask
What did you notice as you tapped and listened? (Sometimes it was difficult to keep counting. The rhythms we heard were different from our tapping. Some of the rhythms did not seem to fit easily with our counting.)

Divide the class into two groups. Group 1 will tap the pulse while group 2 say the words, which replicate the first syncopated rhythm the kartal plays. Next, group 2 clap and say the words, then just clap the words. (You can hear the effect on **reference track 2**.)

	1	**2**	**3**	**4**
Group 1 tap				
Group 2 say	pine—ap-ple and	cheese	on	brown bread
and clap				

Swap over. With the class, devise some new patterns for one group to clap while the other group claps the pulse. Now let the children work in pairs, clapping the pulse and syncopated rhythm together. Encourage the children to devise their own syncopated patterns to clap while their partners keep a steady pulse. When they are ready, let them share their ideas with the rest of the class. Finally, repeat the activity with contrasting untuned percussion instruments, eg. finger cymbals and drum.

long • short • rhythm • pulse • beat • metre • silence

Unsquare dance

What you need to know about the music

Composer: Dave Brubeck (born USA 1920).

Dave Brubeck and his jazz quartet were very popular in the fifties and sixties when Brubeck experimented with combining ideas from western classical music with the complex rhythms of African folk music and the freedom of jazz improvisation. Like many of his pieces, *Unsquare dance* has an odd-number metre – the pulse is grouped in sevens. Eight beats in the metre would have given a more regular feel to the music but, in Brubeck's words, the music 'refuses to be squared'. Brubeck plays the piano solo and the percussionist plays fast syncopated rhythms, tapping his sticks on the side of the bass drum. Two musicians clap a syncopated ostinato which interlinks with the double bass ostinato and continues throughout the piece.

Activity 1

Sevens

The children explore counting different metres.

What you will need
– a drum or wood block

Start the activity by getting everyone to count together in twos.
(Tapping the drum will help to keep the beat steady.)

Count	1	2	1	2
Drum				

Repeat, this time clapping on all the number ones – the strong beat of each group.

Count	1	2	1	2
Clap				

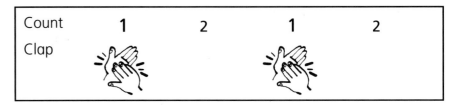

Repeat the counting and clapping with groupings of three, then four and so on up to seven. Try this at a variety of speeds but remember to keep each speed steady.

Count	1 2 3 4 5 6 7	1 2 3 4 5 6 7
Clap		

Repeat the activity from the beginning, choosing an extra number to clap on with each grouping. The two examples below can be heard on **reference track 3**. Notice how to bring the children in together by first counting one cycle of the number group at the speed you want the children to perform.

Count	1 2 3 4 5	1 2 3 4 5
Clap		

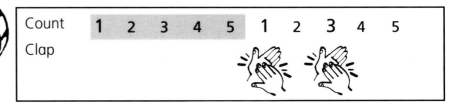

Count	1 2 3 4 5 6 7	1 2 3 4 5 6 7
Clap		

Activity 2

Unsquare ostinatos

The children will learn the rhythm of the bass ostinato and the syncopated clapping ostinato used in *Unsquare dance*.

What you will need
– enlarged photocopies of cards 1, 2, and 3

Listen to track 5 Unsquare dance

The children count quietly in sevens as they listen to track 5 (**reference track 4** shows you how to do this). The music is quite fast so the children may need to listen more than once.

Listen again, noticing the clapping pattern this time. There are several claps in each sequence of seven counts. Can the children identify which numbers are clapped? (2, 4, 6, 7.)

Listen again, asking the children notice what else they can hear in the music. (A double bass plays a repeating pattern which fits together with the clapping pattern. The player plucks the strings with the fingers of the right hand. This playing technique is called pizzicato – pit-zih-**kah**-to.)

Can the children say on which numbers the double bass plays? (1, 3 and 5.)

Learning the rhythm of the bass ostinato

Divide the class into two groups: Group 1 will count while you and Group 2 will tap heels. Show them card 1. Numbers 1, 3 and 5 are the strong beats on which the bass ostinato is played, and on which Group 2 tap heels. Set a slow count to begin with and count one group of seven to bring everyone in together. (**Reference track 6** demonstrates card 1.) Swap over.

Card 1: bass ostinato

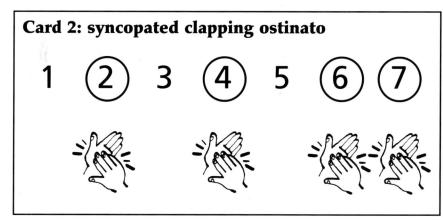

Card 2: syncopated clapping ostinato

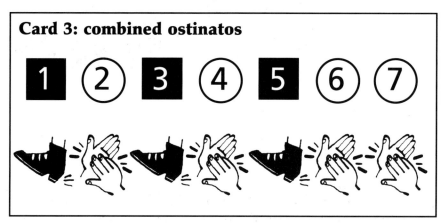

Card 3: combined ostinatos

Unsquare dance

Learning the syncopated clapping ostinato

Now show the children card 2. Group 1 will count in sevens while you and group 2 clap the ostinato. (**Reference track 7** demonstrates card 2.) When this is secure, swap over.

Combining the ostinatos

Now combine the bass ostinato with the clapping ostinato. Group 1 taps heels, group 2 claps – both groups count. Swap over. (**Reference track 8** demonstrates card 3.) When the children are confident with this, encourage them to count silently and memorise the ostinatos.

Now every child taps and claps both ostinatos at the same time.

> ### Listen again to track 5 Unsquare dance
>
> Now the children can hear the combined ostinatos they have learned to play.
>
> *Questions you might ask*
> *What is the difference between our bass ostinato and the one we hear played by the double bass? (We are tapping our heels, the double bass plays different notes – a melody.)*
>
> On a second listening, you might encourage the children to sing the bass ostinato while quietly clapping the other ostinato.

Extension 1 Learning the melody of the bass ostinato

In this extension, groups of children will learn to play the bass ostinato on tuned instruments.

What you will need
– bass xylophone (one or two) or the lowest sounding xylophones you have, keyboards or chime bars, notes GA CDE
– copy of bass ostinato grid (page 9)

G A   C D E

Show the grid to the children. In small groups, the children practise playing this 6-line ostinato on the tuned instruments. (You can hear the ostinato played twice on **reference track 9**.) When the groups are confident, ask each to play while the rest of the children in the class add the clapping pattern (card 2).

Activity 3

Sevens improvisation

In small groups the children take individual turns to play a solo of improvised (made up) rhythms over the combined ostinatos.

> ### Listen again to track 5 Unsquare dance
>
> Ask the children to notice what else they hear in the piece.
>
> *Questions you might ask*
> *What other instruments are played and in what order? (Piano, drum sticks on the metal rim of the drum, then piano again.)*
> *What do you notice about the piano when it plays? (It repeats each of its rhythms several times using different notes.)*
> *What do the sticks play? (Fast tapping rhythms over the ostinatos.)*

What you will need for each group
– tuned instruments as in extension 1
– one pair of drum sticks and a wood block or small drum

Each group needs one or two children to perform the bass ostinato throughout. The other children clap the syncopated ostinato and take turns to improvise rhythms on the wood block with the sticks. Choose a leader to give a count of seven to start the playing.

After one complete bass ostinato is played, the child with the sticks will begin to improvise some rhythms as the others continue to play and clap. While the bass ostinato is played again, the next child comes into the circle ready to play the wood block. Continue until everyone in the clapping group has had a turn (you can hear a version of this on **reference track 10**).

Bass ostinato grid

1	2	3	4	5	6	7
A		G		A		
A		G		A		
D		C		D		
A		G		A		
E		D		E		
A		G		A		

Extension 1

Work out a new bass ostinato using the same numbers on the grid, but changing the notes. Play *Sevens improvisation* with this new bass ostinato.

Extension 2

Devise two linking number patterns like the bass and clapping ostinatos from *Unsquare dance*. Work out a way to write down these rhythms. Add a solo improvisation.

9

Inspector Morse

What you need to know about the music

The composer, Barrington Pheloung, wrote this in 1991 for the title music of the television crime series, *Inspector Morse*. The music begins and ends with an electronic bleep which sounds like the dashes and dots of morse code. The rhythm is taken up by the violins which continue repeating it throughout the piece.

Activity 1

Di daa di daa

In this activity the children will discover how to communicate simple messages using short and long vocal sounds. They will send and receive signals, encode and decode using morse notation.

What you will need
– an enlarged photocopy of the morse code chart (page 12)

> **Listen to track 11 Inspector Morse**
>
> *Questions you might ask*
> *What do you hear at the very beginning of the piece? (An electronic signal, morse code.)*
> *Do you hear this rhythm again? (Yes, it is played all the way through. The electronic bleep comes back at the end.)*
> *Which instruments play this rhythm? (String instruments, eg. violins.)*
> *Does it change at all? (The rhythm stays the same but it is played as a melody.)*

Explain to the children that morse code is a language made up of only two sounds – one short and one long – which are written as a dot and a dash. Each letter of the alphabet has a corresponding code of up to four units, so that whole words and sentences can be formed from just two basic sounds. To distinguish between the letters and words there is always a short silence between each letter and a longer silence between each word.

> **Listen to reference track 12 Morse code letters**
>
> Show the morse code chart to the children. Read through some of the letters with them using *di* and *daa* sounds. Listen to track 12 which demonstrates a selection of letters. There is a gap in which the children can copy each signal.

Now tell the children you are going to spell a word in morse. They will write down each pattern of dots and dashes and then decode it using the morse code chart. Remember to leave a short silence between each letter.

Say:	di di di di	di	di daa di di	di daa di di	daa daa daa
Write:	• • • •	•	• — • •	• — • •	— — —
Decode:	H	E	L	L	O

Try again with some more simple words.

When the children are familiar with the idea, ask them to work in pairs taking it in turns to relay a simple message in morse vocally to their partner, who writes it down and decodes it. **Reference track 13** gives the children an example which they can start with.

Clue: __ _e_ __ __ __ __ / __ _e_ __ __ __.

Activity 2

Secret agents

In this activity, the children learn a song, each line of which ends with finger clicks. Later in the activity, the children replace the clicks with simple morse code patterns.

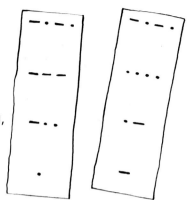

What you will need
– enlarged photocopies of the morse word cards (page 12)

Teach the children the song using **reference track 14**. Each line is repeated so that the children can copy it. (The melody is written in staff notation for music readers at the back of the book.)

Communication, ★ ★ ★ *(finger clicks)*

It's the name of the game, ★ ★ ★

Signalling morse code across the world, ★ ★ ★

Electronic bleepers spelling every word. ★

Communication, ★ ★ ★

It's the name of the game, ★ ★ ★

Talking's good, a message to a friend, ★ ★ ★

Ready now, di daa di daa, about to send. ★

When the children are familiar with the song, explain that in place of the finger clicks at the end of each line, they will say a morse letter (the letters make up a four-letter word).

Divide the class into two groups. Group 1 performs the first verse and first morse word card. Group 2 performs the second verse and morse word card. Practise saying the morse letters with each group before adding them to the song. (There is a complete version of this for you on **reference track 15** followed by a backing track for the children to sing with.)

Now each group will take it in turns to be secret agents and crack the code of the opposite group. Group 1 performs the first verse while group 2 writes down the dot and dash signals. Now Group 2 sing the second verse while Group 1 notate. Afterwards, the words are decoded and revealed.

In smaller groups the children can devise their own four-letter word rhythms. Nominate spies to 'crack' the codes.

Extension 1

Listen again to track 11 Inspector Morse

Can the children write down the pattern of dots and dashes which is repeated throughout, and decode the word? This is not easy. The answer is:

— —   — — —   •—•   •••   •

Extension 2

Use the idea of a repeating morse code rhythm as a background to a melody in group compositions.

Explore instruments to find ways of producing a long and a short sound for playing morse code signals, eg. piano key held down or quickly released, metal instrument held in open or closed hand.

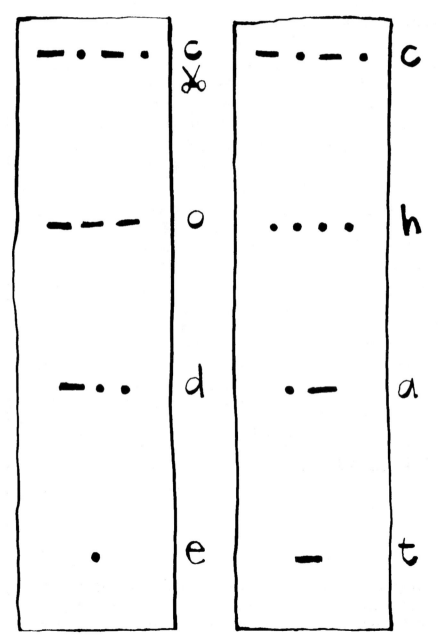
Inspector Morse

Morse word cards

− − • − •	c ✂
− − −	o
− • •	d
•	e

− − • − •	c
• • • •	h
• −	a
−	t

Morse code

a	• −	n	− •
b	− • • •	o	− − −
c	− • − •	p	• − − •
d	− • •	q	− − • −
e	•	r	• − •
f	• • − •	s	• • •
g	− − •	t	−
h	• • • •	u	• • −
i	• •	v	• • • −
j	• − − −	w	• − −
k	− • −	x	− • • −
l	• − • •	y	− • − −
m	− −	z	− − • •

12

DYNAMICS

What you need to know about dynamics

Dynamics in music means volume – degrees of loud and quiet. When they write out their music, composers often include dynamic markings to indicate to the performers how the volume should change.

In many cultures, music is taught by ear and not from written notation. Traditional music is passed on through generations in this way. Dynamics are used, but instead of written markings, an aural signal, such as a rhythm played on a drum, may direct the players to change volume.

Baris gede 'bandrangan' is a modern piece of Balinese gamelan music based on a traditional form. Many types of gamelan music include strong contrasts of dynamics. The players learn their parts by ear and, in this example, they follow signals given by the drummer to change to a different volume. In this piece, there are several very quiet sections alternating with very loud sections, and sections in which the volume increases.

Listening links with the other recordings

After the work on *Baris gede 'bandrangan'*, compare and contrast it with these two pieces.

Listen to track 31 Five pieces for orchestra, no 1

The composer uses only two dynamics throughout: *pp* (*pianissimo*) – very quiet, and *ppp* – as quiet as possible.

Each of the instruments plays single notes or very short melodies at the quietest dynamic they can produce.

Questions you might ask
How would you describe the dynamics? (Very quiet.)
Do any of the instruments play very loudly? (No.)
What is the effect of the quietness? (It sounds calm, gentle, peaceful, sleepy.)

To play quietly, a trumpeter has to use a device called a mute which is placed in the bell of the instrument. Explain this to the children and help them pick out the sound. The trumpet plays the first note of the piece (with the harp) and the penultimate note.

Listen to track 18 Winds on the mountain

Changing dynamics
The piece is in three sections. The chart opposite shows overall dynamics for each section. On a large blank version of the chart, ask the children to indicate which dynamic markings they would choose for each section. Before listening, familiarise them with the possibilities:

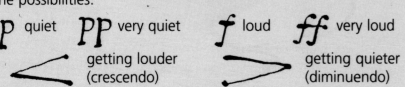

first section	second section	third section
P → PP → ending: < > <	f → >	PP → >

Discuss their choices. Talk about the changes of dynamic within each section, and compare and contrast the sections with each other. (They may notice more detail than in the chart above.)

loud • quiet • getting louder • getting quieter

13

Baris gede 'bandrangan'

What you need to know about the music

Composer: I Wayan Beratha, Indonesia.
Baris gede 'bandrangan' is a modern piece of gamelan music from Bali, composed in 1990, but based on a traditional form. *Gamelan* is the name of the group of instruments (mainly tuned percussion) as well as the music itself.

Gamelan music is an important part of Indonesian life, used for entertainment, at social events and in religious celebration. The traditions of playing go back many centuries and every year competitions are held in Bali to determine the best regional gamelan. Most gamelan have about twenty players, but some are much larger.

A *baris gede* is a ritual spear dance for men; this one is called 'bandrangan' after the tassel attached to the spear's handle. A baris traditionally has a cycle of eight beats repeated throughout.

Activity 1

Listen to track 16 Baris gede 'bandrangan'

This piece lasts fifteen minutes. Only the beginning and end are heard here. Focus the children's attention on the strong contrasts and changes of dynamic in the music as they listen. Afterwards discuss the effects:

● In the first extract, the drums can be heard just before the first melody is introduced. This melody is repeated many times, sometimes played loudly and sometimes quietly.
● The melody comes back in the second extract after a very fast percussion section. It is played quietly at first then grows suddenly louder (crescendo), signalled by louder drumming.
● The last two times the melody is played it becomes gradually quieter (diminuendo) and slower to end the piece.

The instruments heard in *Baris gede 'bandrangan'* are:

- metal gongs of various sizes (above)
- metal bars on a frame, also various sizes (opposite)
- a hand-held cymbal and
- a drum played with a stick (opposite)

Activity 2

Stand up sit down

In this game, the children recognise and respond in movement to aural signals of loud, medium and quiet. It can be played by the whole class grouped in threes.

What you will need
– a drum or tambour and beater
– an area in which the children can move freely in threes

First teach the game to the class. Tell them there are three signals: **loud for stand, medium for kneel, quiet for sit.**

Tap the drum loudly three times; each group of three should respond by all standing up. Tap quietly three times; all sit.

Now tap the drum three times – loud, medium, quiet – and ask them what they think this might be telling them to do. (It means stand, kneel, sit.) Make up different sequences of loud, medium and quiet taps and ask the children to find ways of grouping themselves to indicate the patterns.

Encourage the players to group themselves quietly and quickly. Give the children turns at signalling – they will quickly discover the need for a clear contrast between the three dynamics.

Baris gede 'bandrangan'

Activity 3

Dynamic drum

In small groups or as a class, the children will learn to play a piece with contrasting dynamics in the style of a baris. A solo drummer will 'conduct' the piece by using the drum to signal changes in dynamics to the players. (**Reference track 17** gives you a version; the signals are spoken as well as played.)

What you will need for each group or the whole class
– one large tambour or any drum which can be played both loudly and quietly
– a selection of high, medium and low-sounding metal tuned percussion with these notes:

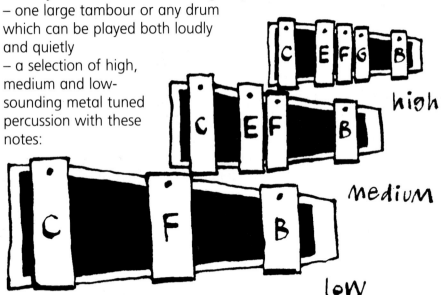

(This is the ideal. If necessary, use whatever you have available with these notes, eg. all medium-sounding instruments, wooden bars, or even a piano.)
– high, medium and low-sounding metal untuned percussion, eg. Indian bells, cymbals, gongs
– copies of the dynamic drum chart (page 17)

The class or each group divides into high, medium and low sections. The players in each section practise playing their sequences of notes from memory, using the syllables of the chant to help them identify when to play. (Untuned instruments in each group may play at the same time as the tuned instruments or may make up their own repeating rhythm patterns.) The children will need some time to prepare the parts separately, and then will need time to practise combining them.

When the children are confident at playing together, choose a drummer who will control the dynamics of the piece by giving a drum signal at the end of each cycle of the melody. To start the piece, the drummer will set the dynamics (and speed) by playing one cycle of eight beats as a solo before the others join in at the same volume. The drummer continues to play throughout, using the three beats at the end of each two cycles of eight, to signal the dynamics for the next two cycles of eight, eg.

● ● ● crescendo or ● ● ● loud all through

The volume may stay the same for any number of repeats, become gradually louder or quieter, or change suddenly.

Listen again to track 16 Baris gede 'bandrangan'

After the activity, ask the children to listen carefully to the drumming as well as the other instruments, noticing the changes in dynamics. Encourage them to use hand signals as they listen to identify –

- sudden change from loud to quiet
- sudden change from quiet to loud
- gradual crescendo
- gradual diminuendo

Questions you might ask
What happens to the music when the drum plays loudly/quietly?
(It becomes loud/quiet.)
How is this similar to our piece of music?

	count	1	2	3	4	5	6	7	8	1	2	3	4	5	6	7	8
high		C	C	E	E	F	G	B	B	B	G	F	E	C			
medium		C		E		F		B		B		F		C			
low		C				F				B				C			
		Ba-	ris	ge-	de	band-	ran-	gan,	this	ba-	ris	band-	ran-	gan			
drum		•	•	•	•	•	•	•	•	•	•	•	•	•	•	•	•
	count	1	2	3	4	5	6	7	8	1	2	3	4	5	6	7	8

TEMPO

What you need to know about tempo

Music can be performed at varying speeds; we can sing a song slowly or quickly, or at any speed in between. In music, the word for speed is tempo.

Whole sections of music often have a constant tempo throughout, neither speeding up nor slowing down. In **Winds on the mountain** the music is organised in three sections: slow fast slow.

In contrast, **Baris gede 'bandrangan'** continuously speeds up and slows down. But as well as hearing changes in the overall tempo of the music, the children will learn that gamelan instruments are played at different speeds according to their size and pitch.

Listening links with the other recordings

Make these links after the activities in the two sections.

Listen to track 35 Dis long time, gal

Sections with contrasting tempos
Explain that this music is in three sections; the melody of each is identical.

Questions you might ask
Does this piece stay at the same speed all the way through or does it change speed? (It changes speed.)
When does the music change speed? (The melody is slow the first time. The second and third times, the melody is fast.)

Listen to track 39 Rondeau from Suite no. 2

Music with a constant tempo throughout
Explain that this music is based on a stately and elegant partner dance of the early eighteenth century. Ask the children to tap the pulse as they listen.

Questions you might ask
Does the tempo stay the same, get faster or get slower during this piece? (It stays the same.)
Can you think of a reason why the tempo needs to stay the same all the way through? (So that the dancers can step together in time with the music. If it got faster, the dancers might not be able to keep in step.)

Music with changing tempos
Compare *Rondeau* with *Baris gede 'bandrangan'*, which is a spear dance for men. How do the children think the changes in tempo might affect the dance movements? How might this dance differ from the *Rondeau* dance? (The movements might vary from slow to fast, be more lively and exciting.)

Winds on the mountain

What you need to know about the music

Winds on the mountain is an instrumental piece based on a traditional South American melody, and performed by the British-based instrumental group, *Incantation*. Change of tempo is a characteristic feature of many types of South American music. Sometimes a piece will consist of a short repeating melody which gradually speeds up and increases in excitement. Other pieces contrast sections of slow and fast tempos as in *Winds on the mountain*.

The melody is repeated in three sections:

- first section – the melody is played first by large panpipes, then by flutes at a slow tempo;

- second section – a change to double speed is signalled by the introduction of the bombo (drum); the panpipes and then flutes repeat the melody at the new tempo;

- third section – the melody drops back to the original tempo again, this time played only by the panpipes.

Panpipes and flutes – the Indian people of the Andes mountains in Chile, Peru and Bolivia have played panpipes and flutes since the time of the Incas. *Sikus* (pronounced **see**-kooss) are panpipes made from several reeds of graduated length bound together. The player blows across the top of the reed. Flutes were made from wood and bone. The *quena* (pronounced **kay**–nah) is a flute made from the thigh bone of the condor.

Stringed instruments – guitars and mandolins arrived with the Spanish in the sixteenth century. The Indians used armadillo shells to make their own version, the *charango* (pronounced as spelt).

Percussion – the *bombo* is a drum made from a hollowed out tree trunk covered with goatskin. *Cha'jchas* (pronounced **chah**–jazz) are rattles made from goats' hooves strung together.

All these instruments can be heard in this piece.

Activity 1

Traffic lights

In this game, the children will explore playing untuned percussion instruments at a variety of speeds, using visual signals. This experience of playing at different speeds will prepare them for responding in a wind dance to the different speeds used in *Winds on the mountain*. The game can be played in small groups or with the whole class.

What you will need
– one enlarged set of the traffic light cards on page 21 (ask a child to colour these red, amber and green as below)
– a selection of untuned percussion instruments (drums, claves, maracas), one per child

Discuss with the children the sequence of colours in a set of traffic lights:

| GET READY | GO | SLOW DOWN | STOP |

Now explain to the children that they may play whatever they like on their instruments (eg. a beat or a rhythmic pattern   at it must be at a speed appropriate to the traffic signals.

at the red and amber signal, begin to play very slowly;

at green there is no speed limit – play as quickly as you like;

on amber, gradually slow down ready to –

stop at the red signal.

One child will be the conductor and will choose when to hold up the cards one at a time in sequence (it may help to number the back of the cards). The conductor may fine anyone who fails to slow down and stop by asking them to miss one turn!

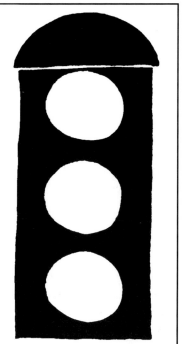
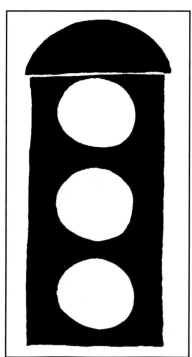

Extensions

In these extensions the children have practice in listening to each other as they play at a variety of speeds. Record the children playing to aid their discussion afterwards.

What you will need
– a cassette recorder
– untuned percussion instruments (one for each child)

1 With two contrasting groups of instruments (eg. wood and metal) and with two conductors play the game again. Each conductor will start and stop their group independently.

Questions you might ask
When did each group change speed? Which group speeded up first? Which group stopped first?

2 In a small group, the conductor holds the cards in sequence as before. This time instead of showing the first card to all the children at once, the conductor shows it to each child one at a time, in any order before going on to the next card.

Questions you might ask
Who was the last person to play fast? Who was the last to stop?

3 In a small group, the players try to make whatever they have chosen to play conform to a common tempo as if they were in heavy traffic and had to avoid bumping into one another. There is no conductor and there are no signals. Because of this the children will need to listen carefully to each other in order to accelerate and slow down together.

Questions you might ask
Did you keep moving at the same speed? What would help you to do this better? (Watching each other as well as listening carefully, changing speed gradually, keeping in control.)

Winds on the mountain

Activity 2

Wind dance

In this activity, the children will first explore then plan a wind dance using different speeds, directions and strengths of movement which correspond with the three sections of the music: slow fast slow. Opposite are some suggestions for movement but the children should preferably find their own.

What you will need
– a large space (a hall)

Listen to track 18 Winds on the mountain

Explain to the children that the music is in three sections. Ask them to respond in movement as they listen to the first section.

Questions you might ask
Does the music in this section change speed? (No.)
How would you describe your movements? (Slow, floating, gentle, smooth, quiet, creeping.)

Now listen and move to the second section

What happened in the second section? (The music was faster.)
How would you describe your movements in this section? (Energetic, lively, stepping, happy, strong.)

Listen and move to the third section

How would you describe your movements this time? (They were similar to those in the first section.)
How would you describe the speeds of the three sections? (Slow, fast, slow.)

Wind dance

Sections 1/3 – slow

Stand still, moving only arms and bodies.

North-south breezes

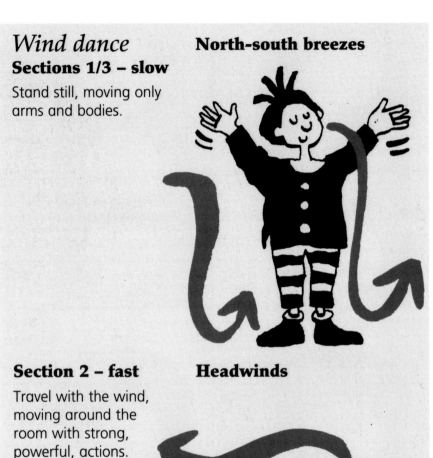

Section 2 – fast

Travel with the wind, moving around the room with strong, powerful, actions.

Headwinds

East-west breezes

Light winds

Warm air waves

Cross winds

Gales

Gusts

Now collect together all the movement ideas for each section and decide with the children which to use in the dance.

Divide the class into groups and let each group choose and synchronise a pattern of movements. Let the groups organise the way in which they want to stand, for instance, they might stand in a circle for the first section and move in a line for the second.

When the wind dance is complete, perform it to *Winds on the mountain* in assembly or for another class.

Baris gede 'bandrangan'

What you need to know about the music

One of the main features of gamelan music (see also page 14) is the way that the gamelan instruments play at different speeds according to their size and pitch. This tempo relationship of the instruments to each other is maintained as the overall tempo speeds up and slows down.

Activity 1

Listen to track 19 Gamelan

In this simplified version of *Baris gede 'bandrangan'*, the tempos of the different instruments can be heard very clearly. The drum signals the start and the overall speed, then is joined in turn by the lowest- to the highest-sounding instruments.

Questions you might ask
Is the lowest-sounding instrument playing fast or slow? (Slow.)
Can you describe the speed of the highest-sounding instrument? (It is fast, it is the same as the drum.)
What do the other instruments do? (They play at two speeds in between the highest- and lowest-sounding instruments.)

Listen to track 16 Baris gede 'bandrangan'

Encourage the children to notice overall changes in tempo as they listen. The whole piece lasts 15 minutes – the beginning and end are heard here. It begins with gongs playing a slow opening. The drum joins in to signal an increase in tempo as the first melody is repeated several times by the whole gamelan. The closing extract shows how the tempo has increased again to create an even more exciting atmosphere. This is exaggerated by the very rapid drumming and cymbal playing. At the very end, the music dramatically slows down as the original melody is played a last two times.

Activity 2

Gamelan

In this activity, groups of children will learn to play the simplified *Baris gede 'bandrangan'* which they heard on track 19 *Gamelan*. When they are confident they may go on to make changes in the overall tempo, eg. moving from slow to fast to slow.

What you will need for each group
– a copy of the gamelan chart and instructions (page 25)
– a cassette recorder
– a drum
– any metal tuned percussion of different sizes with these notes:

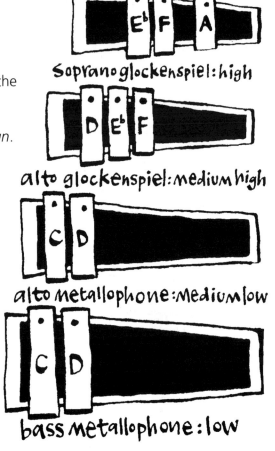

soprano glockenspiel: high

alto glockenspiel: medium high

alto metallophone: medium low

bass metallophone: low

Give the gamelan chart to the children and let them work out the patterns for themselves. The syllables of the chant will help them identify when to play.

The children will decide how to put the patterns together and how many times they will play. They may choose to play the bass pattern first and then add the others one by one as on track 19, or they may prefer to start in a different order, or all together. The drummer will direct the tempo by tapping a steady beat.

Count	1	2	3	4	5	6	7	8	1	2	3	4	5	6	7	8
high	F	F	F	F	A	A	A	A	F	F	F	F	E^b	E^b	E^b	E^b
medium high	D		D		D		E^b		D		E^b		F		E^b	
medium low	D				C				D				C			
low	C								D							
	ba-	ris-	ge-	de	band-	ran-	gan,	this	ba-	ris-	ge-	de	band-	ran-	gan,	this
drum	•		•		•		•		•		•		•		•	

1. Choose one part each. The lowest-sounding (largest) instruments play the bottom line, the highest-sounding (smallest) play the top line.

2. Choose a drummer to count and tap twice from 1 to 8 slowly and steadily while you each practise your line on its own.

3. When you can all play your parts over and over again without a mistake, try putting them together. You will need to decide how you will do this. Start at the bottom, adding one part at a time? Start together? Start at the top? Which works best?

4. When you can play together, try playing the whole piece faster or slower with the drummer setting the speed. Can you speed up or slow down gradually all together?

5. Record what you have played then listen to it. Decide how you would like to change it for a final performance. Think about:

• how to begin
• how many times each player will play
• when you will change speed and how
• how it will end

25

TIMBRE

What you need to know about timbre

Every sound has its own unique quality – this is timbre (taam-br). (The term *tone* may also be used.) Even though two sounds may be equally high or low, and may last the same length of time, we can discriminate between them if their timbres are different.

Everyone's voice has a timbre of its own, enabling us instantly to recognise friends and family by sound alone. Every different type of instrument has an individual timbre – think of the clear difference between the sound made by the wooden bars of a xylophone and the metal bars of a glockenspiel.

Within one instrument there can be a range of timbres, often affected by the way the instrument is played – a drum played with a beater sounds different from the same drum played with the hands; the string of a violin when it is played with the bow sounds very different from the same string plucked with the fingertip.

The children will compare two versions of **La Volta** and hear how the same melody, played at the same speed and on the same notes, sounds different because it is played on different instruments.

1

lute
Viol   Violin

2

harpsichord
recorder

In **Tomorrow the fox,** there are many contrasts of timbre. The piece starts with unaccompanied voices and the timbres of the individual female and male voices can clearly be heard. This is followed by a rousing instrumental section performed here on authentic Elizabethan string and wind instruments which have a particularly 'rustic' timbre.

The piece continues, alternating instrumental sections with voices and instruments combined, and every so often the instruments suddenly stop and the voices are heard alone again.

Listening links with the other recordings

These links examine more closely the timbres of music from the other sections. Listen to them after exploring timbre in this section.

Listen to track 42 Kartal

Questions you might ask
What material do you think the instrument is made of?
(Wood.)
How do you think it is played (see page 60)?
(It sounds like something being tapped.)
Are there any classroom instruments which would make a similar sound?
(Claves, wooden castanets, wooden sticks on a wood block or table top.)
Which words describe this sound?
(Clicking, clacking, tapping.)

Listen to track 31 Five pieces for orchestra, no 1

In this piece, Webern has used instruments of the orchestra in a way which highlights their individual timbres. Sounds pass from one instrument to another and it is possible to hear the different tone qualities clearly. The piece is very short so the children will need to listen several times.

Questions you might ask
Can you identify any of the instruments? (Flute, glockenspiel, harp, trumpet, violin, clarinet are all featured and some children may be familiar with them.)
Can you describe any of the sounds? (At the beginning the glockenspiel plays three notes on its own. The flute plays a 'fluttering' sound made by rolling the tongue while playing. This is called 'flutter-tonguing'. The violin and clarinet both play very high-pitched notes. All of the sounds are light and quiet.)

Listen to track 37 Didlan

Tell the children they will hear singing, and they will try to notice how many voices they hear. They will try to identify the types of voices by their sound quality (timbre).

Questions you might ask
Did all the voices start together? (No.)
How many voices were there? (Three.)
Who do you think were singing: men, women, girls or boys? (One woman and two men – one man had a much deeper voice than the other.)

Listen to track 18 Winds on the mountain

Ask the children to listen to the first slow section of the piece and think about the instruments they hear.

Questions you might ask
How do you think the first two instruments are being played?
(The first is blown; the second has strings which are strummed with the fingers – see page 19.)

Do the sounds remind you of any instruments you have heard or played before? (Flute, blowing over the tops of milk bottles or plastic tubes, and guitar, ukulele or banjo.)

Which instrument plays the melody next? (A flute.)

Now listen to the whole of the fast second section.

Which new instruments can you hear? (A drum and rattles.)

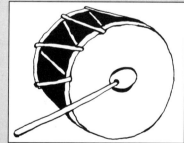

Listen again, noticing the sounds of the bombo and cha'jchas. (The drum signals the change from the slow to fast section and plays a dull thudding pulse throughout the middle section. The cha'jchas are heard throughout, occasionally making a fast rippling effect, clearly heard at the end of this section.)

smooth • rough • hard • ringing • sparkling • shiny

La Volta

What you need to know about the music

The *volta* was a court dance which became extremely popular for a short period at the end of the sixteenth century. It was only danced by the younger and more energetic ladies and gentlemen (including Queen Elizabeth I), because it contains high jumps and turns by both partners as well as a move in which the woman is lifted and turns in the air. The name of the dance (from the Spanish, *voltear,* to throw up in the air) refers to these moves.

Because the melody for the dance would have been played by whatever instruments happened to be available, the timbres changed accordingly. In the first version of the music for the dance (track 20), a violin plays the melody, accompanied by a lute and a viol. The lute and the viol repeatedly play the same notes throughout, which is a form of accompaniment called a drone.

The recorder plays the melody in the second version (track 21), accompanied on a harpsichord playing a repeating pattern of three different notes – an ostinato.

Lute – a many-stringed instrument used extensively in Elizabethan times. The strings are plucked with the fingertips.

Viol – one of a family of bowed string instruments of varying sizes. The violin and viol families developed at around the same time in the early 1500s, but the viol family dropped out of popularity 250 years later.

Violin – basically the same instrument then as it is now – a four-stringed instrument, played with a bow.

Harpsichord – a keyboard instrument which predates the modern piano. The strings are plucked by quills rather than being struck by hammers as in the case of the piano.

Recorder – very much the same instrument as today's, the recorder was very popular in Elizabethan households.

lute

viol

Violin

Activity 1
Performing La Volta

In this activity, the children will compare the two versions of *La Volta*, noticing differences in instrumental timbres. Groups will then learn to play the melody and devise accompaniments on a variety of instruments using drones and ostinatos. Sample versions are given on **reference track 22**, but the aim is to allow the children to take decisions about combinations of timbre as they develop their own arrangements. You may need to introduce the melody and each of the drones and ostinatos to the whole class before they work in groups.

harpsichord

recorder

Listen to tracks 20 and 21 La Volta

Ask the children to complete the table below (a blank photocopiable table is given on page 32), which will help them to compare the two versions of the piece:

La Volta	Same	Similar	Different
Melody (tune)	✔		
Tempo (speed)	✔		
Dynamics (loud/quiet)		✔	
Melody instruments			✔
Accompaniment instruments			✔

Questions you might ask
Which instrument played the melody in each version? (Violin then the recorder.)
Can you describe the accompaniment in each version? (In the first a string instrument, lute, was strummed like a guitar. The rhythm changed but the same notes were played all the way through – a drone. In the second, we heard a repeating pattern of three notes on the harpsichord – an ostinato. Sometimes the harpsichord copied the recorder's melody.)

La Volta

Performing La Volta *(continued)*

What you will need

– cassette recorder

– **melody**: a variety of tuned instruments such as recorders, xylophones, keyboards, violin, and a melody card or staff notation (see back cover) for each player

–

drones: chime bars G and D, glockenspiel, guitars, keyboards and a drone card for each player

– **ostinatos**: tambours, drums, Indian bells, tambourines, xylophone, and an ostinato card for each player

Divide the class into small groups, each with one or two children who will play the melody. (The children playing the melody may choose the easier option of playing the first half only, see below, which they can keep repeating as often as they like. Music readers may prefer to play the complete melody which is given at the back of the book.)

The remaining children will explore the timbres of different combinations of instruments and consider their suitability for accompanying the melody instruments in their group.

They may:

● play any or all drones

● play any or all ostinatos

● play a mixture of drones and ostinatos

● make up their own patterns on the ostinato card

The children should consider carefully the effect of different combinations of timbres by recording and listening to their choices.

When each group has completed an arrangement of the piece, share it with the rest of the class, comparing the timbre effects created by their choices of instrument and accompaniments.

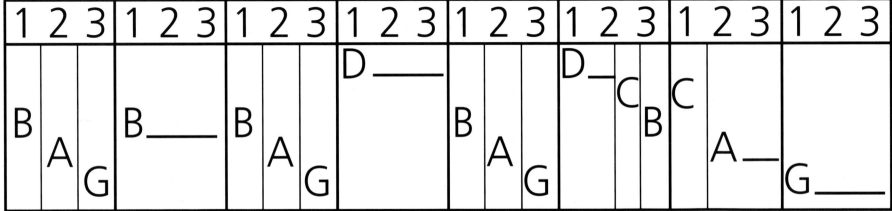

La Volta melody - easy version.

La Volta drone card

Choose an instrument, then count quietly to yourself as you repeat the drone over and over again:

Chime bars – strike both bars together on 1:

1   2   3   1   2   3

Keyboard – play notes D and G together on 1:

1   2   3   1   2   3

Guitar – strum the chord of G on every count:

1   2   3   1   2   3

Glockenspiel – play G, or G + D, on each count:

1   2   3   1   2   3

La Volta Ostinato Card

Choose an instrument then count quietly to yourself as you repeat the ostinato over and over again:

Tambour/drum – strike once on each count:

1   2   3   1   2   3

Tambourine – tap this pattern:

1   2   3   1   2   3

Indian bells – tap this pattern:

1   2   3   1   2   3

Xylophone – strike one note on each count:

1   2   3   1   2   3

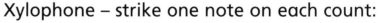

La Volta

La Volta	Same	Similar	Different
Melody (tune)			
Tempo (speed)			
Dynamics (loud/quiet)			
Melody instruments			
Accompaniment instruments			

Table for comparing the two versions of La Volta

Tomorrow the fox

What you need to know about the music

Composer: Thomas Ravenscroft (c1590 – c1635).
This song dates from the time of Elizabeth I, although its melody, *Trenchmore*, was written in Henry VIII's time. It was common at this time to write new words to existing popular tunes already familiar to the public. In 1609, Ravenscroft published two of the earliest collections of English printed songs. Many of these were rounds and included probably the first printed version of *Three blind mice*. Although he was a learned church musician, he was determined to write music for all tastes: for 'court, city and country'. Another more practical reason for publishing collections of popular and part-songs was that he was unable to make a living from church music alone.

Tomorrow the fox is a rousing country, or 'rustic', ballad. It contrasts strongly with *La Volta*, which is typical of the more elegant court music of the same period. The song would have been performed in taverns and outdoors, so the voices are accompanied by instruments which have a particularly powerful timbre:

Tambourine – originally a Middle Eastern instrument, and little changed in 800 years, it was introduced into Europe during medieval times.

Cittern (**sih**-tern) – a pear-shaped instrument with metal strings which are plucked or strummed.

Bass curtal (**kuhr**-tal) – a double reed wind instrument similar to the bassoon.

Treble rebec (**reh**-bek) – a small pear-shaped, bowed string instrument used particularly for song and dance music (can be heard playing the melody in the instrumental sections).

tambourine

Cittern

bass curtal

treble rebec

Activity 1

Match up voices

In this game, the children explore their voices to produce different tone qualities (timbres). Play the game on different occasions, encouraging the children to be more imaginative each time they play it.

What you will need
– space to stand in a circle

All together clap twice, then shake hands in the air twice to a steady beat:

One by one around the circle, the children now say their names during the two shakes and everyone repeats the names during the next two shakes.

clap clap Da-niel clap clap Da-niel

When the children can do all this confidently, ask them to disguise their voices when they say their names. Everyone will try to copy each solo voice, matching the sound as closely as possible. (You will have some inventive and hilarious results.)

Questions you might ask
What was (Nasreen's) voice like? (Squeaky, growling, smooth.)
Whose voice was hard to copy? Why?

33

Tomorrow the fox

Activity 2

Match up memory

This is a memory game for individuals, groups or the whole class. The players will learn to recognise the timbres of a variety of instruments played on tracks 23-26, then identify the missing instrument in the four questions which follow in each track.

What you will need
– copies of the instrument strips opposite and an answer chart below

Draw a picture or write the name of the missing instrument in this chart:

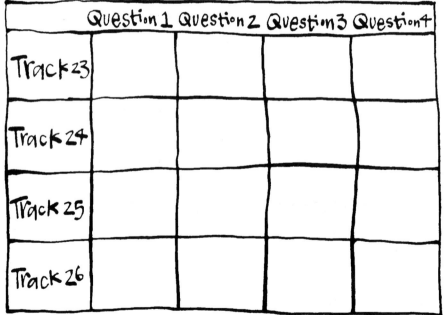

	Question 1	Question 2	Question 3	Question 4
Track 23				
Track 24				
Track 25				
Track 26				

Answers – the missing instruments are:
Track 23 – Question 1 Cow bell. 2 Tulip block. 3 Tambour. 4 Castanet. **Track 24** – 1 Recorder. 2 Lute. 3 Violin. 4 Harpsichord. **Track 25** – 1 Panpipes. 2 Tin whistle. 3 Mouth harp. 4 Tamboura. **Track 26** – 1 Curtal. 2 Tambourine. 3 Rebec. 4 Cittern.

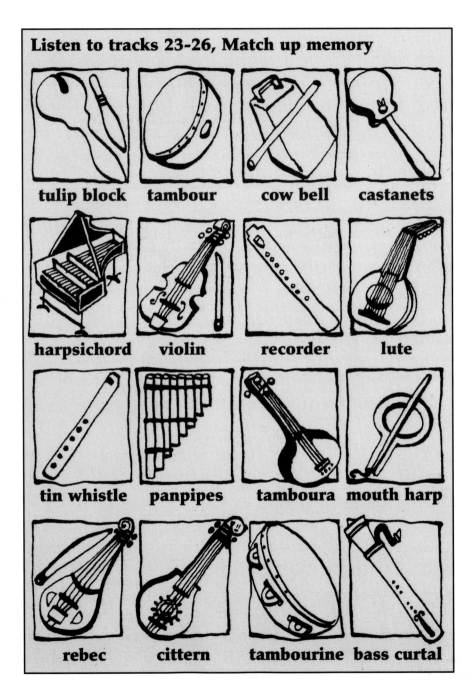

Listen to tracks 23-26, Match up memory

tulip block   tambour   cow bell   castanets

harpsichord   violin   recorder   lute

tin whistle   panpipes   tamboura   mouth harp

rebec   cittern   tambourine   bass curtal

Activity 3

Singing Tomorrow the fox

The children will learn to sing *Tomorrow the fox* and in subsequent activities explore, distinguish and select a variety of instrumental timbres to use in devising accompaniments to and links between the singing.

What you will need
– copies of the song sheet opposite

Teach the song to the class using **reference track 27** (staff notation is given at the back of the book for music readers). The first verse and chorus are given with gaps after each line for the children to copy. Then the instruments play the whole song so that the children may sing along.

1   Tomorrow the fox will come to town
    Keep! keep! keep! keep! keep!
    Tomorrow the fox will come to town
    Oh, keep you all well there.

Chorus   I must desire you neighbours all
    To hallow the fox out of the hall,
    And cry as loud as you can call:
    Woop! woop!
        woop! woop! woop!
    And cry as loud as you can call,
    Oh, keep you all well there.

2   He'll steal the hen e'en from the pen!
    Keep! keep! keep! keep! keep!
    He'll steal the hen e'en from the pen!
    Oh, keep you all well there.

3   He'll steal the lamb e'en from the
        dam!
    Keep! keep! keep! ...

4   He'll steal the duck e'en from the
        brook!
    Keep! keep! keep! ...

Activity 4

Scrap band sort out

The aim of this activity is to explore and distinguish between the timbres of a range of environmental sound-makers. The children will sort the sounds in a singing game, and then use their knowledge to distinguish between them in a listening exercise.

What you will need
– a sound-maker for each child from a collection of four different materials: paper, wood, plastic, metal, eg.

- newspaper, tissue paper, crinkly wrapping paper
- off-cuts of wood, chopsticks, wooden spoons, twigs
- plastic pots, spoons and tubs
- metal spoons, ladles, washers, biscuit tins

Say the words of the first verse of *Tomorrow the fox* to the children as a chant. Now ask everyone to copy the rhythm of the words on their sound-makers playing all together:

       etc

To-mor-row the fox will come to town ...

Questions you might ask
What did it sound like when we all played together? (You will get a mixture of responses: some may have liked the loudness, others may not have been able to hear their own sound.)

Now sing this version of the song which will group the instruments into their different materials. (You can hear a performance of this on **reference track 28**, followed by a backing track for the children to sing and play along with.) Afterwards, discuss the results with the children. What do they notice about the sounds produced by instruments made of the same materials? Can they identify them played behind a screen?

Scrap band sort out

All sing verse 1:
Tomorrow the fox will come to town
Keep! keep! keep! keep! keep!
Tomorrow the fox will come to town
Oh keep you all well there.

You sing (verse melody repeated):
I must desire you neighbours all
To hallow the fox out of the hall,
And cry as loud as you can call:
Metal all well there.

All metal instruments play the verse 1 rhythm.

All sing verse 1 again:
Tomorrow the fox will come to town ...

You sing:
I must desire you ...
Wood all well there.

All wood instruments play the verse 1 rhythm ...

Listen to track 29 Paper, plastic, wood, metal
The children will hear three short pieces of music which combine the different timbres of paper, plastic, wood and metal. Can they identify the materials and describe how they think the sounds are being made?

Activity 5

Tomorrow the fox finale

The children select three instrumental timbres to represent the hen, lamb and duck of the song. Encourage them to consider the different ways they can play to achieve the timbre they want.

Listen to track 30 Tomorrow the fox

Questions you might ask
What do you hear in the first verse and chorus of this song? (Male and female voices – no instruments.)
When the instruments play first, are they alone or playing with the voices? (Alone – they play a link after the chorus.)
Can you describe the sounds of any of the instruments and say how they might be played? (The children should be able to pick out a high-pitched, bowed string instrument, a gruff bass line played by a blown instrument, and a tambourine.)

What you will need
– a selection of classroom instruments

Divide into three groups to perform one verse each by singing it and playing the rhythm of the words at the same time. For fun and extra effect the children can sing in a vocal timbre which characterises their animal.

Activity 6

Something old, something new

Choose a favourite song and write new words for it, as Thomas Ravenscroft did with *Tomorrow the fox*, then devise a performance using voices and instruments with a variety of timbres. Here is one idea for you to try.

Ask the children to suggest new words for *She'll be coming round the mountain*, then collect suitable sound-makers, eg.

She'll be riding round the mountain on a bike ... *(play a bell in the gap after each line)*

She'll be clomping round the mountain wearing clogs ... *(wood blocks)*

She'll be skipping round the mountain in the spring ... *(bird whistles/springs)*

She'll be floating round the mountain like a ghost ... *(spooky sounds)*

Sing the new verses, adding sound effects to the end of each line. Perform your 'new song' to another class or at assembly.

| **All sing verse 1 and chorus** | **Hens sing and play** | **All sing chorus** | **Lambs sing and play** | **All sing chorus** | **Ducks sing and play** |

TEXTURE

What you need to know about texture

Sounds can be used singly or in any variety of combinations – this is texture. Texture can be as thin as the sound of a solo voice or as thick as a large orchestra all playing together. Often the texture changes within a piece of music, adding to the interest.

Five pieces for orchestra, no1, although written for orchestra, is unusual in that the texture is very thin. Brief, separate fragments of sound are heard in a very clear, open texture. Instruments play singly one after the other at the beginning and end of the piece, whilst the middle section has a very slightly thicker texture as the instruments briefly combine or overlap.

Dis long time gal is a traditional Jamaican song arranged for steel band. The children will hear a variety of musical textures as sections of the band play singly and in combination.

Listening links with the other recordings

Explore the textures in these pieces after the activities on *Five pieces for orchestra, no 1* and *Dis long time, gal.*

Listen to track 37 Didlan

Ask the children to notice how the texture changes in this piece. It starts with a single voice which is joined by a second and then by a third.

Later in the piece the texture thickens again as more voice parts are added.

Dee dee dee diddle
Dee dee dee diddle
Dee dee dee diddle

Listen to track 30 Tomorrow the fox

This song is performed in this recording by a group of singers with instrumentalists providing a contrasting texture.

Questions you might ask
What do you hear at the beginning of this piece? (Singing – a female voice and male voices singing together.)
After the first verse and chorus what happens? (The voices stop and we hear a group of instruments.)
There are three main textures in this piece. Can you say what they are? (Voices only, instruments only, and voices with instruments.)

verse 1 and chorus	link	verse 2 and chorus	link	verse 3 and chorus	link	verse 4 and chorus	ending

Listen to track 5 Unsquare dance

This piece has four sections, each with a different musical texture. The texture changes as four sounds are combined in various ways. These sounds are hand clapping, double bass, piano, and tapping with sticks on the side of a drum.

Photocopy the blank chart below. As the children listen to the music they complete the chart. This will illustrate the changes of textures. They will need to listen several times to check their answers. (The answers are opposite.)

	Section 1	Section 2	Section 3	Section 4
Bass drum			✔	
Grand Piano		✔		✔
clapping	✔	✔	✔	
Double bass	✔	✔	✔	

	Section 1	Section 2	Section 3	Section 4
Bass drum				
Grand Piano				
clapping				
Double bass				

thin • thick • solo • chorus • one sound • several sounds

39

Five pieces for orchestra, no 1

What you need to know about the music

Composer: Anton Webern (born Vienna, 1883–1945). Webern composed this set of five pieces in 1913, each one a miniature lasting a minute or less. No 1 is titled 'Sehr ruhig und zart' – very calm and delicate. Webern uses tiny fragments of melody, chooses the instruments of his orchestra for their distinctive timbres, then weaves the sounds together in a very open texture. The composer, Stravinsky, a contemporary of Webern, likened his music to 'dazzling diamonds', and indeed Webern seems to treat each sound like a unique, precious gem.

Beginning – the harp and (muted) trumpet, celeste, flute and glockenspiel play single sounds one after the other making a very thin texture.

Middle – this is made up of combinations of different sounds, making the texture slightly thicker.

End – glockenspiel, harp, flute, trumpet and finally celeste play one by one mirroring the very thin texture of the beginning.

Activity 1

Listen to track 31 Five pieces for orchestra, no 1

Listen several times with the children. It may help them to concentrate if they close their eyes.

After they have heard the piece a few times, discuss their reactions to and ideas about the music. Collect together the words they use to describe the music and a list of any scenes they imagine as they listen. (Keep these for the extension activity on page 42.)

Questions you might ask
What mood was the music – calm, gentle, strong, exciting, mysterious, happy, lonely?
Did you imagine any pictures or stories as you listened?
What words would you use to describe the sounds?

Activity 2

Night music

In this activity, the children make a piece of music with a musical texture similar to that created by Webern.

What you will need
– a wide variety of different instruments – enough for each child to choose one for its special sound quality. (The illustration of instruments opposite suggests the type of range you might aim for. If a wide enough range of classroom instruments is unavailable, supplement with environmental sound-makers.
– a cassette recorder
– copies of the word picture opposite

Night Music

Night

DARK

quiet

Cold

Peace

Still

Calm

Sleep

Five pieces for orchestra no. 1

Night music (continued)

Enlarge the *Night music* word picture on page 41 and show this to the children.

Reading from left to right, notice how there are individual words at the beginning and end of the picture. The middle section overlaps in a complex scene.

Beginning and end

Choose eight children and allocate one child to each of the eight words – night, dark, quiet, cold, calm, still, peace and sleep. Each child will then select a sound which they think suggests their word. They will need time to try out different ideas on the instruments. When they are ready, listen together to the thin texture of each chosen sound played one after the other.

Middle

Allocate one feature of the picture to small groups of the rest of the class. They are:
moon, stars, space, trees, reflections, shadows, reeds, water.

Within their groups, each child selects a sound which suggests their part of the picture, and then the whole group tries out combining and ordering the individual sounds into a texture of their choice. How the texture of the middle section is further developed will depend on the conductor.

Performing *Night music*

Now, the final texture of the piece takes shape. An appointed conductor brings in the sounds by pointing to them on the picture as the signal for the children to play:

- Beginning and end – word sounds are played one by one as the conductor points to each in turn

- Middle – the conductor points to the parts of the picture which should be played separately or in combination. The conductor can bring groups back in in different combinations, let them be heard once only, all together – there are many different texture options.

Use a cassette player to record the result and discuss the textures with the children. Give other children turns to conduct alternative versions.

> ### Listen again to track 31 again
>
> Ask this question before the children listen.
>
> *How is this piece similar to the piece of music we made? (All the sounds are quiet. Both pieces use a lot of different instruments. The instruments play only a few sounds each. The sounds are heard one by one at first, then several sounds together in the middle section, then one by one at the end.)*

Extension

Ask the children to create a new picture with a new texture using the words they suggested when they first listened to *Five pieces for orchestra, no 1*. Use the picture as a plan for a new composition. This can be a whole class, group or individual activity.

Dis long time, gal

What you need to know about the music

This piece is based on a traditional Jamaican song, here arranged for and performed by a junior school steel band. On track 35 the children will hear the verse and chorus melodies of the song played three times, each time with a different musical texture.

First verse – the piece opens with the melody played in unison (everyone playing the same) by the tenor pans – a thin-sounding texture.

First chorus – the same tenor pans are divided into two groups playing in parallel with each other.

Second verse and chorus – the bass pans play a very short section on their own, then the texture thickens as the tenors and cellos join in.

Third verse and chorus – the texture is further thickened by the addition of percussion.

Bass pans

Tenor pans

Cello pans

Dis long time, gal

Activity 1

Listen to track 32 Steel pans

The objective is to familiarise the children with the sound of the different steel pans. On track 32, they will hear five extracts drawn from the arrangement of *Dis long time, gal*:

Extract 1	the tenor pans play the verse melody slowly
Extract 2	the tenors divide into two parts to play the chorus melody and a part which moves in parallel with it
Extract 3	the cellos play the verse and chorus melody at a lower pitch
Extract 4	bass pans begin, joined by all the tenors playing an accompaniment to the melody which is not heard
Extract 5	bass pans play the bass line alone

Ask these questions before the children listen to the music (they may need to listen several times). Refer them to an enlarged copy of the picture of the instruments on page 43.

When can you hear the melody played on its own? (In extracts 1 and 3.)
Which pans do you think played each time, and how do you know? (Extract 1: the tenors because they are the smallest pans and make the highest sound. Extract 3: the cellos because they make a lower sound but not as low as the basses.)
Which pans do you think played the last extract? How do you know? (Bass pans because they are the largest and make the lowest sound.)
What can you hear in extract 4? (Bass pans play, then different groups of tenors play an accompaniment. None play the melody.)
Why is extract 2 different from extract 1? (The tenors play in two groups.)

Activity 2

One two many

This game can be played by a group of children or the whole class. The children will play a chosen rhythm in a variety of musical textures using body percussion and later transferring the game onto untuned percussion instruments.

First make up a rhythm. Fitting words to it may help the children to memorise the pattern. Here is an example, which you can hear on **reference track 33** (the words are from *Dis long time, gal*):

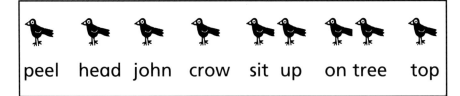

peel   head   john   crow   sit   up   on tree   top

Practise clapping the rhythm with the children in the way shown on track 33 until they can clap it from memory without the words.

Now choose a conductor to stand where everyone can see. The conductor will use four signals:

 one index finger pointing to one person: one person performs

 both index fingers pointing to two people: two people perform

 all fingers pointing to everyone: everyone performs

 stop signal to everyone: silence

Each player will now perform the rhythm, *Peel head john crow sit up on tree top*, using their own choice of body percussion. They begin when signalled and keep repeating it until the signal moves to other players. (There is a version of the game on **reference track 34**, in which the signals are given vocally.)

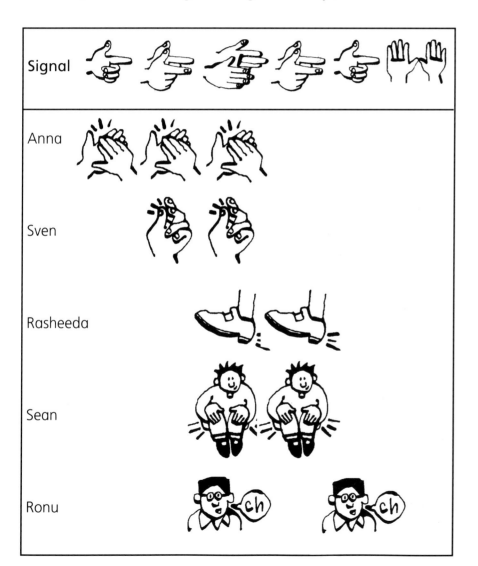

Rules

1. The game always starts with signal 1, but after that the signals can be used in any order until the game ends with the stop signal.

2. When the conductor uses signals 1 and 2 he or she should point at individual players.

3. Once signalled to the players keep repeating the rhythm until the signal moves to someone else.

After one round of the game, discuss the variety of textures with the children. (Explain that a solo is when one person plays alone.)

Questions you might ask
Who played on their own – a solo?
When two people played together, were they using different body sounds or the same to play the rhythm?
What was the effect when the whole group played together? (It was much louder, there were lots of different sounds – stamping, clapping, clicking, tapping – all playing the rhythm at once.)
Which texture was the thinnest? (The solo.)
Which was the thickest? (When everyone joined in.)

Listen to track 35 'Dis long time, gal

Questions you might ask
How is the texture of this piece similar to that of the game we played? (At first we heard one melody, then there were two playing together. When the melody was repeated there were lots of instruments playing.)

Listen again.

When you hear two parts, are they playing the same rhythm or do they have different rhythms? (The same.)

Dis long time, gal

Activity 3

Texture twist

This is an activity for individual children. The aim is to recognise the changes of texture in track 35 *Dis long time, gal,* and to place strips representing the texture in the correct running order, which is shown below.

What you will need
– a photocopy of the texture strips on page 47 and a pair of scissors (the children need to cut out the texture strips)
– a cassette recorder or CD player
– track 35 *Dis long time, gal*

Activity 4

One two many with instruments

The children will play the same game as in activity 2, but on instruments instead of body percussion. Encourage the conductors to think about interesting textures of sounds they might achieve as they choose one, two, or all of the players.

What you will need
– untuned percussion instruments (you may decide to use one per child, or if the group is large, distribute a selection so that children can take turns using instruments and body percussion)

As the children become familiar with the game, each new conductor may also choose a new rhythm. Discuss the different sequences of textures which are produced in each game as the conductors use the signals in different ways.

Activity 5

A new twist

This is an activity for small groups. The children will use the texture strips on page 47 in an order of their own choice to make up a new piece of music.

What you will need
– one set of texture strips per group
– different types of tuned instruments, eg. recorder, kazoo, xylophone, keyboard, swanee whistle
– some untuned percussion instruments

The children will need to find a new interpretation for each strip. They may like to use a known melody in place of '*Dis long time, gal,* or compose their own.

Texture Strips

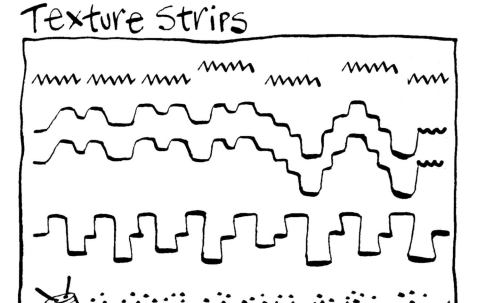

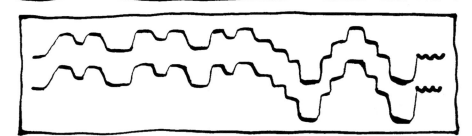

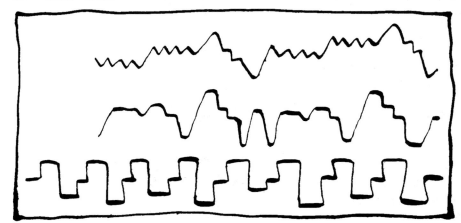

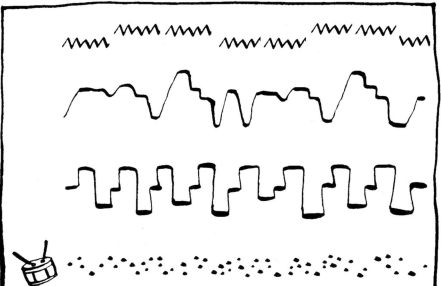

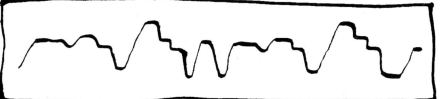

PITCH

What you need to know about pitch

Sounds in music can range from low to high – this is what is referred to as pitch.

Our voices can produce more than one pitch, but the total range of notes we can sing comfortably is determined by whether we are male or female, and by our age. The ranges of the voice are given special names. The most common are:

soprano – high (children and women)
alto – medium to high (children, women and some men)
tenor – medium (men)
bass – low (men)

As a general rule, larger instruments produce lower pitches. For example, a large drum will make a lower sound than a small drum of a similar type.

Didlan is sung by three unaccompanied voices: one female and two male voices of different pitch; soprano, tenor and bass.

Stamping tubes is played on bamboo tubes of different lengths and diameter, which each produce one pitched sound. Several players play together to provide a range of pitches.

Listening links with the other recordings

Explore these links before or after the rest of the section.

Listen to tracks 20 and 21 La Volta

Ask the children to notice the accompaniment to each version.

Questions you might ask
Version 1: does the accompaniment stay on the same pitch, move higher or move lower? (It stays the same.)
Version 2: can you describe the pattern of pitches you hear in the accompaniment. (There are three pitches which jump up from low to medium to high again and again.)

Listen to track 18 Winds on the mountain

Listen to the whole track and compare the pitch of the three sections.

Questions you might ask
Would you describe the pitch of the panpipes which play the melody at the beginning of the piece as high or low? (Low.)
Do the next two sections sound the same general pitch or different? (The fast section sounds mainly high, the last is low.)

Listen to track 36 Winds on the mountain pitch shape

The melody of *Winds on the mountain* is in four short phrases (like four phrases within a sentence). Ask the children to draw with their hands in the air the pitch shape of the first phrase:

Questions you might ask
Does the phrase move step by step or in jumps? (It jumps.)

What do you notice about the next phrase of six notes? (It is very similar to the first, but it starts at a slightly higher pitch.)

What do you notice when the flutes play the melody later in the first section? (The pitch moves even higher.)

Didlan

What you need to know about the music

Didlan is performed by Plethyn (pleh-**thin**), a Welsh folk group. They have taken the well-known Welsh folk song, *The Ash Grove*, and arranged it for three unaccompanied voices (ie. without instruments). They do not sing the traditional words, but instead sing nonsense words, 'dee dee dee diddle', rather as we do when we have forgotten the words of a song.

The melody is sung by the female singer all the way through the piece. The children will hear this voice alone before the higher of the two male voices, the tenor, joins in singing a harmony part under the melody. Thirdly, the lowest voice, the bass, adds a bass part underneath the two upper parts.

In the second section, of the music more parts are added by recording the singers' own voices together with the original three parts.

Activity 1

Pitch in

In this game, the children will explore their own vocal ranges by singing a well-known song, starting at a different pitch each time: low, medium and high.

What you will need
– three chime bars of different pitch, eg. A E B. (If chime bars are not available use any pitched instrument, eg piano – A below middle C, E and B above.)

Choose a simple tune that everyone knows well, eg. *Frère Jacques*. Instead of singing the words ask the children to suggest some nonsense sounds they can sing, eg. *zee zee zee zee*, or *da da da dum*.

- Strike the middle chime bar, E, and sing the song using this as the starting note.
- Repeat, this time starting on the highest-sounding bar, B.
- Go back to singing at the middle pitch again.
- Now try the lowest-sounding bar, A.

Questions you might ask
Which version sounded highest/lowest?
Was it easy to sing all three ways – high, medium and low?
If not, which one was most comfortable for our voices? (Individual children may have different preferences.)

Listen to track 37 Didlan

Explain to the children that they will hear a song. The words of the song will be nonsense words.

Questions you might ask
What do you hear first? (A woman's voice.)
Do you hear any instruments? (No.)
How many other singers can you hear? (Two men.)
Who has the highest voice? (The first singer, the woman.)
Whose voice is lowest? (The third singer's.)

Didlan

Activity 2

Singing snakes and ladders

This game gives the children the opportunity to use their voices at different pitches in a variety of ways. Play it together as a class at first. Later it can be played in small groups or pairs.

What you will need
– an enlarged copy of the game picture
– one or two dice
– two xylophones or other instruments with these notes (these will help the children pitch the notes for squares 3 and 13):

Extensions

After playing *Singing snakes and ladders*:

1 Ask the children to design their own class or individual boards. Remember – on each square they must do something with the pitch of their voices.

2 Play the game using a tuned instrument, eg. play each task on a xylophone or recorder instead of singing.

kes and Ladders

A G F E D C B A -een eight- -ber num- to up climbed I **Sing**

limb up the ladder step by step **14**

Sing 'The wheels on the bus' in a wobbly voice as you go over the bumpy road **17**

← slide down a long snake

Slide down a small snake **16**

C B A G F E D C step top the to -der lad- the up **Sing**

Climb up the ladder step by step **4**

In 'London's burning' which word has the highest note? **7**

go up slowly on the ski lift and ski down the mountainside **6**

Sing a song which moves up at the beginning **5**

PITCH

Rules of the game

1. To start the game choose a song and sing it in your normal voice.

2. Throw the dice to move.

3. When you land on a square, follow the instructions to make sounds with your voice, eg. make your voice do a curvy slide down the snake shape from high to low.

4. The winner is the first to arrive at number 20 - give yourself three cheers!

51

Stamping tubes

What you need to know about the music

This piece of music is from the Solomon Islands in the Pacific Ocean where 'bamboos of the ground' – stamping tubes – are played for entertainment.

Each bamboo tube is a different length and diameter and so produces a different musical pitch. The musicians hold two tubes in each hand and strike the open ends on a large, smooth stone.

In this piece, three young women play a total of twelve stamping tubes to create an exciting effect of patterns in which the combinations of pitches can clearly be heard.

Activity 1

Tapping tubes

In this activity, the children will investigate the relationship between size and pitch.

What you will need
– a collection of cardboard or plastic tubes of different lengths and diameters (open-ended foil inner tubes or poster tubes)
– several tappers (cut ovals of corrugated card about 15cm long by 10cm wide)

Choose about five tubes of different sizes. Give one tube and one tapper to each of five children. Ask each child in turn to tap one end of their tube while the rest of the class listen carefully. Can the listeners line up the five players in order of pitch from the lowest-sounding tube to the highest?

Questions you might ask
Whose tube made the lowest sound?
Why? (It is the longest and/or widest.)
Whose tube made the highest sound?
Do you notice anything about the size of this tube? (It is the shortest and/or narrowest.)

If possible, let the children experiment in small groups, finding out and recording their results using:

● five different lengths of tube cut from the same diameter
● five different diameters of tube of the same length

When they have placed their tubes in order of pitch, ask them to make up some simple music and devise a way of writing it down so that another group can interpret and perform it.

When writing their music down, they might for example:
- number the tubes and write a number code for the players
- colour the tubes and write a colour-coded chart

They may also like to try the music below for three pitches. Give the children the score without suggesting an interpretation

initially, as they may happily work out their own ideas. If they need direction, suggest these choices:

- play one sound per symbol.
- play one repeating pattern per symbol.
- play freely whenever your symbol appears (appoint a conductor).

Tapping tube trio

rule: don't play in the empty spaces

Stamping tubes

Activity 2

Pitch walls

In this activity, groups of three children work out a series of simple pitch patterns and write them down on pitch walls. They play their patterns using instruments of three contrasting pitches: high, medium and low.

What you will need
– three sound-makers of different pitch for each group, eg.
  ● three plastic tubs: small, medium and large
  ● three drums: small, medium and large
  ● three xylophone bars: short, medium and long
– photocopies of the blank pitch walls on page 55

Step 1
Teach the class this chant.

Child 1	Can you play this rhythm?
Child 2	I can play this rhythm.
Child 3	I can play this rhythm.

Now ask each group to repeat the chant as follows:
  ● child 1 in a high voice,
  ● child 2 in a medium voice,
  ● child 3 in a low voice.

Show the children what this looks like on a pitch wall:

	high	child 1: Can you play this rhythm?		
	middle		child 2: I can play this rhythm	
	low			child 3: I can play this rhythm

Step 2
Ask the groups to perform this version of the chant which alters the pitch pattern:

	child 1: I can play this rhythm	child 1: I can play this rhythm
child 2: Can you play this rhythm?		child 2: I can play this rhythm
	child 3: I can play this rhythm	child 3: I can play this rhythm

Step 3

Introduce the instruments. Repeat steps 1 and 2 with each group playing their chosen instruments to the rhythm of the chant words.

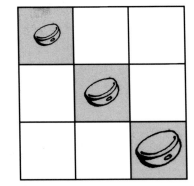
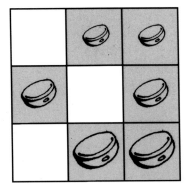

Step 4

Ask the groups to devise their own pitch patterns using the same rhythm. They may like to work them out by playing first then writing them down on a pitch wall when they are satisfied, or write them down, then play to see whether they like the results.

Listen to track 38 Stamping tubes

Questions you might ask
At the very beginning what is the order of pitch of the first three sounds you hear? (High, low, medium.)
Do you hear this pattern again? (Yes, it is repeated many times, but with other sounds added.)
After the music stops briefly in the middle of the piece what do you notice about the pitch? (It changes, there are some higher sounds.)

Extensions

Give this set of suggestions to each group of three children.

1 Play your pitch wall several times:

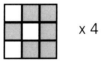 x 4

2 Use more than one pitch wall.
Decide how many times to play
each wall:

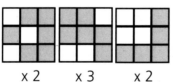

x 2   x 3   x 2

3 Choose your own rhythms (making up some words may help you to remember it).

4 Join up with another group to play your pitch walls together:

x 5

x 5

5 Build a long pitch wall by putting together the patterns from several groups. Each group will play their pieces in turn, reading the grids from left to right.

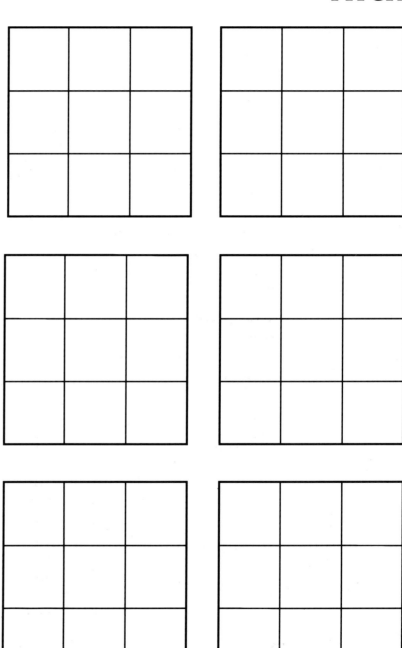

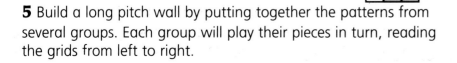

STRUCTURE

What you need to know about structure

Music can be structured in a variety of ways. As we listen to a piece of music we become aware of repetitions and patterns, and of combinations of different sounds which together make a coherent whole. Sometimes sections of music are organised in a simple, regular structure, which we can readily recognise as we listen, eg. the A and B sections of binary form, the ABA sections of ternary form, or the ABACA sections of rondo form. (*Structure* and *form* are interchangeable terms.)

In other pieces of music the sounds may not be grouped in these regular arrangements and we may at first be less aware of how they are ordered.

In addition, all music is made up of varied combinations of its elements – duration, timbre, texture, dynamics, pitch, tempo – and it may be the way in which these are used which gives a piece its shape and form. Through **Rondeau** and **Kartal**, the children will be exploring rondo form and how to consider the elements within this structure.

Listening links with the other recordings

Explore these binary and ternary structures before or after *Rondeau* and *Kartal*

Listen to track 18 Winds on the mountain, tracks 21–22 La Volta, and track 5 Unsquare dance

All of these pieces are in ternary form (ABA). Ask the children to listen to the pieces one at a time and identify the difference between the A and B sections.

Winds on the mountain
The melody is repeated but the tempo changes:

A slow	B fast	A slow

La Volta
The melody changes in section B:

A first melody	B second melody	A first melody

Unsquare dance
After an ostinato introduction (double bass and clapping) there are three sections in which the instruments change.

A piano	B drum	A piano

Listen to track 30 Tomorrow the fox and track 32 Dis long time, gal

Both these pieces are in binary form (AB), familiar to children through the many songs which have two main sections – a verse (A) and a chorus (B). Ask the children how they can recognise the difference between the verse and the chorus in each piece.

Dis long time, gal
The melodies of the verse and chorus are different.

Tomorrow the fox
Verse words change, chorus words are repeated.

Ask the children to compare verse 1 with verse 2 in each piece and tell you what they notice?

Dis long time, gal
The melody of verse 2 is played on lower-pitched steel pans than those in verse 1, and the tempo is faster.

Tomorrow the fox
Verse 1 has voices only, verse 2 has voices and instruments.

Explore these different types of structure after *Rondeau* and *Kartal*.

Listen to track 16 Baris gede 'bandrangan'

One of the characteristic features of gamelan music is the vertical layering of long and short sounds. The tuned instruments are grouped according to their pitch, each playing their own versions of the melody at different speeds. Those with the lowest pitch play the melody very slowly with long, sustained sounds. Each higher group plays their version of the melody progressively faster. The effect is of many layers of long, in-between and short sounds.

Ask the children to listen to the piece and try to pick out some of the different versions of the melody. (All of the patterns fit into two cycles of eight counts with the lowest-sounding instruments playing on counts 1 and 5 and the main melody playing on each count.)

Questions you might ask
What else do you notice as you listen to this music?
(Sometimes the tempo changes and all the instruments play faster. There are often changes in dynamics with a loud section repeated very quietly. Sometimes we can hear different groups of instruments playing. The drumming is very clear at certain points and stops at others.)

Listen to track 11 Inspector Morse

Questions you might ask
How has the composer organised the sounds in this piece?
(It begins with a repeating electronic morse code rhythm pattern – an ostinato – which continues all the way through the music, played by the violins at different pitches. A melody is added to the ostinato and we hear more instruments of the orchestra as the melody repeats. At the end of the piece the electronic signal returns.)

Listen to track 31 Five pieces for orchestra, no 1

The structure is possibly less obvious than in any other example. There is no repeating melody which we can easily hum or repeating ostinato we can quickly recognise. The dynamics throughout are quiet and we cannot hear a pulse. It is so brief, the piece has ended before our ears have become adjusted to the sounds. But with repeated listening it is possible to understand that the choice and order of sounds is very deliberate.

Webern's intention to create a 'very calm and delicate' miniature for orchestra led him to select a particular series of sounds, each for its own distinctive timbre. Although played by instruments of the orchestra, many of the sounds are unusual eg. the trumpet plays with a mute (see page 13). The sounds are played individually or combined together in an airy, open texture.

Questions you might ask
What do you like about this piece?
How is it different from some of the other pieces we have listened to?
Do you think the composer has been successful in creating 'a very calm and delicate' piece of music?

beginning middle end • repetition • contrast

Rondeau

What you need to know about the music

Composer: Johann Sebastian Bach, born Eisenach (1685–1750). Bach's *Rondeau* (the French spelling of rondo) is the second of seven pieces in his *Suite no 2* for orchestra. Bach was one of several composers of his time who composed suites – each one a group of short listening pieces based on dances popular across Europe. His *Rondeau* gives the impression of a stately and elegant court dance.

Bach's orchestra for this suite consists of:

– a small number of strings – violins, violas, cello, double bass
– solo flute
– harpsichord

As you listen to track 39 *Rondeau*, try to pick out the orchestral features listed below to identify the different sections: **AABACA**. This will enable you to help the children recognise them.

Activity 1

Rondeau dance

In this activity the children will learn simple dance steps for the **A** section of the rondo and devise steps for the **B** and **C** sections.

Listen to track 39 Rondeau

Ask the children to listen to the piece all the way through once.

Questions you might ask
What did you notice about the first melody you heard in this music? (It kept coming back again.)
Did you hear any other melodies? (Yes, they were in between.)

Listen again, asking the children to raise a hand each time they hear the repeating melody of the **A** section, and lower it during the **B** and **C** sections. It may help if they sing the **A** melody.

 The whole orchestra plays. The melody is played by flute and violins. The cello, double bass and harpsichord play a bass line under the melody.

The dance

One step left, one step right,
Swing hands up then swing them down,
Swing hands up then swing them down.
One step left, one step right,
Swing hands up, let go, then turn
    around.

 Repeat of first A

The dance

Repeat the first A steps.

 At the beginning the harpsichord and lower strings drop out.
At the end a melody is played by the cello.

The dance

Children make up their own steps to contrast with the A section.

What you will need
– a large space, eg. a hall

Learning the A section dance steps

In small groups the children form circles holding hands. On **reference track 40** you will hear the steps called out for each line of the melody. Call the instructions out as the children learn the steps, or as they practise with the music (the aim should be for the children to dance the steps, not sing them).

Making up the B and C section dance steps

Working in their small groups, the children devise their own steps for sections **B** and **C** to contrast with section **A** (you are given an example of **B** section steps on **reference track 40**). (Note that section **B** has six phrases of music, section **C** has eight.)

They will need to be very familiar with the music to do this, and ideally should have their own access to the recording.

Let each group perform their complete dance, **AABACA**. Finally perform all the dances at the same time. Each group's **B** and **C** sections will differ, but during the **A** section all of the groups will dance the same steps, emphasising the structure of the music.

Listen again to track 39

Ask the children to notice, as they listen, any additional elements, which help us identify the different sections, eg.

A – the melody is repeated at the beginning of the piece so we quickly recognise it. The texture is thickest in this section.

B – at the beginning the texture is thinner and the timbre changes as the lower strings and harpsichord drop out.

C – the music is mainly quiet. The timbre of the flutes, upper strings and harpsichord is heard at the beginning, followed by a thinner texture when the harpsichord drops out.

 Repeat of first A

The dance
Repeat the first A steps.

 The flute starts this section with a running step by step melody. At the end, the harpsichord and lower strings stop playing until the return of section A.

The dance
Children make up their own steps to contrast with the A section.

 Repeat of first A

The dance
Repeat the first A steps.

Kartal

What you need to know about the music

Kartal is the name of the percussion instrument heard in this piece of music from Rajasthan in Northern India. The instrument consists of four rectangles of thin hard wood, about 15 x 5cm. The player holds two in each hand and with great skill claps them together to produce complex and rapid rhythms, twirling arms and hands at the same time. Kartal, like those illustrated below, are available through musical instrument suppliers; these often have finger holes and sometimes metal jingles attached.

The structure of the piece can be described as a very free rondo:

A – a rhythm pattern, based on a unit of four counts, is firmly established at the beginning. It is repeated ten times.

B – a different rhythm pattern interrupts.

A returns.

C, D, E etc – several more contrasting patterns follow, always alternating with **A**. These contrasting patterns become increasingly exciting as the player demonstrates his skill. The original **A** rhythm does not return at the end of the piece.

Activity 1

Rhythm rondo

This is a circle game in which the players perform a body percussion pattern (**A**), and improvise contrasting clapping patterns (**B, C, D** etc). The structure is:

A B A C A D A and so on.

What you will need
– space for the children to sit in a circle

A – this is a repeated section in which everyone plays the same body percussion pattern.

B C D E – in these sections individual children contribute their own rhythm patterns while the others shake hands in the air four times.

First teach this repeated pattern:

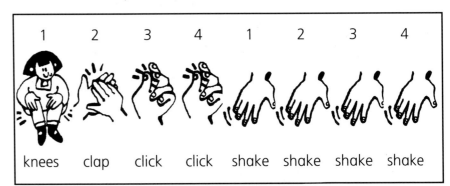

1	2	3	4	1	2	3	4
knees	clap	click	click	shake	shake	shake	shake

Keep repeating over and over again, counting out loud at first, then silently in your heads.

Now ask some children to volunteer each to improvise in turn a clapping pattern during the four silent shakes (there is an example for you on **reference track 41**).

Activity 2

Concentration rondo

In this activity, the children learn a chant (**A** section) to add to the body percussion from *Rhythm rondo*. While the body percussion continues throughout, individual children add words on a chosen subject to make contrasting sections (**B**, **C**, **D**, **E** etc). This can be played round the class or by small groups in circles.

When everyone can perform the body percussion and chant confidently, agree on a number of subjects for the contrasting sections. To help you all remember them, list them on a board. During these sections, individual children will take it in turns to say the name of one example of the chosen subject, fitting it into one cycle of the body percussion. If anyone repeats a word already contributed, or cannot supply a new word, everyone returns to the **A** section at the beginning of the next cycle of body percussion. (**Reference track 43** gives you a sample of the game.)

The last **A** section finishes on 'keep in rhythm, words to find.'

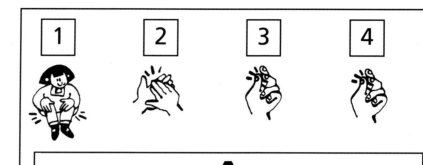

| 1 | 2 | 3 | 4 |

A

Con – cen – tra – tion,

Con – cen – tra –tion, use your mind.

Keep in rhy – thm,

Keep in rhy – thm, words to find.

Subject:

Insects!

B

Bee!

Moth!

Beetle!

Um ... (Return to A)

Kartal

Activity 3

Animal elements rondo

In this activity, one group of children will transfer the rhythms of the body percussion of activities 1 and 2 into a tuned percussion ostinato. Another group will transfer the words of *Concentration rondo* onto instruments to form an **A** section. Six other groups will compose music for six contrasting sections featuring one set of animals and one musical element each:

A – duration: birds
B – dynamics: African animals.
C – tempo: river and pond life
E – timbre: insects
F – texture: sea creatures
G – pitch: nocturnal animals

What you will need
– ostinato group: low-pitched instruments, notes C D G.
– A section group: tuned instruments with notes C D E G A
– animal elements groups: enough untuned or tuned instruments for all, and one bell (eg. indian bells or cow bell)

Teaching the ostinato

Remind the children of the *knees clap click click* pattern, then replace the body percussion with the notes C, D and G:

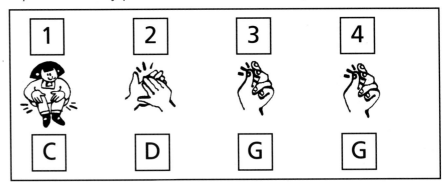

Repeat the ostinato throughout and play it on its own twice at the beginnin...

62

Teaching the A section

Remind the children of the *Concentration rondo* chant, then replace the syllables of the chant with the notes C D E G A.

C		D		G		G
Con	–	cen	–	tra	–	tion,

A	C	G	C	E	D	C
Con –	cen –	tra –	tion,	use	your	mind.

C		D		G		G
Keep		in		rhy	–	thm,

C	D	E	G	E	D	C
Keep	in	rhy –	thm,	words	to	find.

The ostinato and A section groups should practise combining their parts: the ostinato group starts the piece by playing two cycles of their pattern, and continues throughout.

Composing contrasting sections

Encourage each group to discuss how to feature their element as they depict their type of animal. The way they choose to organise their compositions can draw on the relevant section of the book, eg. duration might use morse-like signals of long and short, texture might be inspired by a word picture. The length of each section may vary, but the end of each must be signalled by striking a gong or bell once.

Encourage each group to devise ways of notating their music, eg. a sound picture (page 41), a chart (page 17), pitch walls (page 55). When the groups are ready to perform, put the whole piece together, using the chart below to remind the players of the sequence.

the piece and on its own once at the beginning of each A section

Index (terms, composers and instruments)

alto (voice), 48

Bach, Johann Sebastian, 58
ballad, 32
baris, 14
baris gede, 14
bass (voice), 48
beat, 4
Beratha, I Wayan, 14
binary form (AB), 56
bombo, 19
Brubeck, Dave, 6

celeste, 40
cha'jchas, 19
charango, 19
cittern, 32
crescendo, 13
curtal, bass, 32
cymbal (gamelan), 15

diminuendo, 13
drone, 28
drum (gamelan), 15
duration, 4
dynamics, 13

flute (orchestral), 40
flute (South American), 19
flutter-tonguing, 27
form, 56

gamelan, 14–15
gong (gamelan), 15

harp, 40
harpsichord, 28

improvisation, 8
Incantation, 19

kartal, 60

loud (f), 13
lute, 28

metal bar (gamelan), 15
metre, 4
mute (trumpet), 13

ostinato, 4

panpipes, 19
pans (tenor, cello, bass), 43
Pheloung, Barrington, 10
phrase, 48
pianissimo, 13
pitch, 48
pizzicato, 7
Plethyn, 49
pulse, 4

quena, 19
quiet (p), 13

Ravenscroft, Thomas, 32
rebec, treble, 32
recorder, 28
rhythm, 4
rondo form, 56

sikus, 19
silence, 4
soprano (voice), 48
stamping tubes, 52
steel band, 43
structure, 56
suite, 58
syncopation, 4

tambourine, 32
tempo, 18
tenor (voice), 48
ternary form, 56
texture, 38
timbre, 26
tone, 26
trumpet, 40

unison, 43

very loud (ff), 13
very quiet (pp), 13
viol, 28
violin, 28
volta, 28
volume, 13

Webern, Anton, 40

Acknowledgements

The following have kindly granted their permission for the use of copyright recordings included on the accompanying recording:

Art of Landscape for **Winds on the Mountain**, performed by Incantation (Simon Rogers, Mike Taylor, Forbes Henderson) from CD NAGE 101 © 1982 Art of Landscape.

BMG Records (UK) Ltd for **Rondeau** from *Orchestral Suite No 2* BWV1067 by Bach, performed by La Petite Bande from CD GD77008 © 1990 Harmonia Mundi Freiburg.

The Decca Music Group Ltd for **Tomorrow the fox will come to town** from 'Music from the Time of Elizabeth I', performed by the Academy of Ancient Music/Christopher Hogwood CD 4331932 Ⓟ 1982 The Folio Society © 1982 The Decca Music Group Ltd.

EMI Records Ltd for **La Volta** performed by David Munrow and the Early Music Consort of London from 'The Instruments of the Middle Ages and Renaissance' HMV SLS 988 Ⓟ 1976 © 1976 and **La Volta** performed by David Munrow with Christopher Hogwood and Gillian Reid from 'David Munrow Introduces and Performs Mediaeval and Renaissance Music' CFP 4384 Ⓟ 1982 © 1982, by kind permission of EMI Records Ltd and the estate of David Munrow.

Harmonia Mundi UK Ltd for *Claquette-Tap dances* (**Kartal**) from Rajasthan and bambous pilonnants from 'Musical Instruments of the World' CD LX274675 (Le Chant du Monde) Ⓟ© 1990.

King Record Co Ltd, Japan for *Gamelan Gong Kebyar of 'Eka Cita'* (**Baris gede 'bandrangan'**) Abian Kapas Kaja from © CD KICW - 1006. Licensed by King Record Co Ltd, Tokyo, Japan.

Sain Recordings Ltd for arrangement of traditional air 'Llwyn Onn' (**Didlan**) by Plethyn (Healy, Griffiths, Gittins) © Cyhoeddiadau Sain 1994, from 'Seidir Ddoe' by Plethyn, Sain SCD 2083 Ⓟ 1994 Sain (Recordiau) Cyf.

Sony Classical for **Orchestral Piece No 1** from *Five Orchestral Pieces Op 10* by Webern performed by the Juilliard String Quartet and the London Symphony Orchestra conducted by Pierre Boulez from CD SM3K 45845 © 1978 Sony Music Entertainment Inc. Used by permission of Sony Classical and Anton Webern, Universal Editions AG (Wien) and Alfred A. Kalmus Ltd.

The Valentine Music Group for **Unsquare Dance** by Dave Brubeck, performed by Dave Brubeck Quartet from CD CRS 32046, © Copyright 1961 by Derry Music Co. USA. All rights for World (ex USA, Canada and Japan) controlled by The Valentine Music Group, 7 Garrick Street London WC2E 9AR.

Virgin Records Ltd for the theme from **Inspector Morse** by Barrington Pheloung © 1991 Central Television Limited, licensed courtesy of Virgin Records Limited.

All other recordings are copyright A & C Black: track 32 and 35 **Dis long time, gal** performed by Dog Kennel Hill Primary School Steel Band; tracks 24 and 26 performed by 'Folies Bergères'; tracks 12, 14-15 and 27-28 performed by Rosamund Chadwick; all remaining tracks devised and performed by Helen MacGregor and Stephen Chadwick.

All rights of the producer and of the owner of the works reproduced reserved. Unauthorised copying, hiring, lending, public performance and broadcasting of this recording prohibited.